BRAZIL

Edward Parker

W
FRANKLIN WATTS

This edition 2012

First published in 2009 by
Franklin Watts
338 Euston Road
London NW1 3BH

Franklin Watts Australia
Level 17/207 Kent Street
Sydney NSW 2000

 Produced for Franklin Watts by
White-Thomson Publishing Ltd
+44 (0) 845 362 8240
www.wtpub.co.uk

Series consultant: Rob Bowden
Editor: Sonya Newland
Designer: Alix Wood
Picture researcher: Amy Sparks

A CIP catalogue record for this book is available from
the British Library.

Dewey Classification: 918.1

ISBN 978 1 4451 0810 0

Printed in Malaysia

Franklin Watts is a division of Hachette
Children's Books, an Hachette UK company.

www.hachette.co.uk

Picture Credits
Corbis: Cover (Gavin Hellier/Robert Harding World
Imagery), 7 (Ben Radford), 9 (Sergio Pitamitz), 14
(Marc Lecureuil), 22 (Paulo Fridman), 24 (Paulo
Fridman), 27 (Robert Maass), 28 (Carlos Cazalis);
Dreamstime: 8 (Tony1), 18 (Mortenelm); **iStock:** 4,
10, 20; **Edward Parker:** 13, 29; **Photoshot:** 15 (WpN),
25 (WpN); **Shutterstock:** 1 (Celso Pupo), 16 (Pres
Panatoyov), 17 (David Davis), 19 (Rafael Martin-
Gaitero), 21 (Vinicius Tupinamba), 23 (Celso Pupo), 26
(Franck Camhi); **White-Thomson Publishing:** 6, 11, 12.

Contents

Introducing Brazil

Brazil is the fifth largest country in the world. It is bigger than Europe, almost 55 times the size of the UK and has borders with all South American countries except Ecuador and Chile. The largest river in the world, the Amazon, runs through Brazil, and it also has the largest area of unbroken rainforest on the planet.

▼ *The statue of Christ the Redeemer towers above Rio de Janeiro, the second largest city in Brazil. The statue has been named one of the New Seven Wonders of the World.*

◀ Brazil has international land borders with 10 of the other 12 South American countries Argentina, Bolivia, Colombia, French Guiana, Guyana, Paraguay, Peru, Suriname, Uruguay and Venezuela.

A global influence for 500 years

Brazil has had global connections ever since the Portuguese explorer Pedro Cabral arrived there in 1500. The Portuguese cut down Brazil's rare trees to extract a dye from the wood, and dug for minerals such as gold and diamonds. Soon, plantations were established to grow crops such as sugar and coffee, and slaves were brought from West Africa to provide labour. The plantations made the Portuguese fabulously wealthy and influenced the development of the European economy.

The rubber boom

Brazil gained independence in 1822, and the Brazilian people began to enjoy their country's wealth for themselves, particularly at the end of the nineteenth century during the 'rubber boom'. The demand for rubber for vehicle tyres was so great that the Amazonian city of Manaus briefly became richer than New York. However, soon after this, the Brazilian economy began to decline. Later, the coffee boom encouraged people from countries such as Italy and Japan to move to Brazil to work.

▲ *Brazil has nearly one quarter of all the fresh water on Earth flowing through it, which gives it great potential for hydroelectricity.*

The BRICS countries

In the 1950s, Brazil began a massive development programme. The Brazilian government borrowed money from wealthy countries to build factories, roads, ports and power stations. Today, it is one of the four most important developing nations in the world; these countries are known together as BRICS, which stands for Brazil, Russia, India, China and South Africa. They have a major influence on the world because between them these countries have huge natural resources and more than a third of the world's workforce. As the BRICS countries develop, they are changing the global economy.

Natural resources

Brazil has a huge wealth of natural resources, including some of the world's largest deposits of iron ore, bauxite (used to make aluminium), diamonds and gold. Production of many of these resources, especially gold, declined in the 1990s, as restrictions on mining in the Amazon were introduced. Recently, though, investment in mining has increased again. Brazil is also the world's largest producer of sugar, oranges and beef. However, the country's development has led to the destruction of large areas of rainforest, contributing to global climate change, which is now affecting the whole planet.

BASIC DATA

Official name: **Federal Republic of Brazil**

Capital: **Brasilia**

Size: **8,511,965 sq km (3,286,488 sq miles)**

Population: **205,716,890**

Currency: **Real**

FAMOUS BRAZILIAN

Pelé
(b. 1940)

Pelé is one of the most famous living Brazilians. He starred in the 1970 and 1974 football World Cup finals, where his brilliance made him a household name around the world. Since retiring from football, he has worked to raise awareness of and find solutions to poverty in Brazil.

Brazil around the world

Brazilian culture has spread around the world and Brazilian communities can be found in major cities from London to New York. Brazilian art, music, literature and architecture are now famous throughout the world. Brazil is famous for introducing the rest of the world to the samba dance, bossa nova music and what many people consider to be the most stylish way of playing football.

◀ *Brazilian football star Kaká is tackled by England player David Beckham. Kaká was named FIFA World Player of the Year in 2007.*

Brazil is a very large country – so large that it covers nearly half of the entire South American continent, and dominates the economy of the region. The Amazon River runs through the rainforest in the north of the country, and Brazil also has 7,491 km (4,655 miles) of Atlantic coastline.

The Amazon area

Brazil is divided into five main regions, each of which has its own distinctive landscape and climate. The largest is the Amazon region. It is an enormous area – more than 3.8 million sq km (1.5 million sq miles) – mostly covered in dense tropical rainforest and dominated by water, with thousands of lakes and rivers.

THE HOME OF...

The Amazon River

Every hour, 773,000 litres (170,036 gallons) of water from the Amazon River pour into the Atlantic Ocean. At 6 million sq km (2.3 million sq miles), the Amazon also has the largest drainage basin on the planet. The Amazon is the second longest river in the world, after the River Nile in Africa, with a length of 6,437 km (4,000 miles).

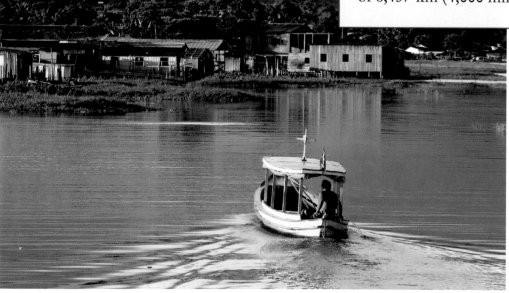

◀ *The Amazon runs through Brazil's rainforest and is the largest river in the world by volume.*

Centre-west

The Centre-west is the second largest region in Brazil. Its main feature is a high tableland, or plateau, called the Planalto, which has an average altitude of 1,000 m (3,281 ft) above sea level. The Planalto is largely covered by the Cerrado – a vast area of scrubland. The region also has major deposits of important metals such as gold and nickel.

PLACE IN THE WORLD

Total area: 8,511,965 sq km (3,286,488 sq miles)

Percentage of world land area: 5.7%

World ranking: 5th

North-east

The North-east region is located south of the Amazon River and includes a large area of semi-desert known as Sertão. This area gets very little rain, so farming is difficult. The coast of the North-east region is famous for its hot weather and beautiful beaches and dunes, which make it a major tourist attraction. The coastal strip of the North-east is ideal for sugar plantations and other tropical crops.

▼ *Tourists enjoy buggy riding among the sand dunes of Genipabu in north-eastern Brazil.*

South-east

The South-east region covers around 10 per cent of Brazil. It is an area of rolling hills with an average altitude of 700 m (2,297 ft) above sea level. This area receives high rainfall and the land is good for large-scale farming. The South-east region has metal and mineral deposits, as well as Brazil's most important oil fields. Industry and services are also important to the economy here. The South-east borders the Atlantic Ocean, and several of Brazil's main cities are located along the coast, including Rio de Janeiro and São Paulo.

▼ *Rio de Janeiro, with its famous natural landmark Sugar Loaf Mountain, is situated on the south-east coast of Brazil.*

South

The South region has gently rolling hills in some areas, which give way to rugged mountains and forested valleys. Some parts of the South are very similar to the Alpine areas of Germany and Italy. The European-style landscape has attracted Italian and German immigrants to cultivate vineyards and set up Brazil's wine industry here. The landscape is well suited to other types of European-style agriculture, including dairy farming to produce milk for the food-processing industry.

Brazil's climate

Brazil's climate is varied. The Amazon region has a very even climate. It is hot and wet all year round, with daytime temperatures averaging 26°C (79°F) and with an annual rainfall of 1,500 to 2,000 mm (59 to 79 in). Most of the North-east coast has a warm, tropical climate, with a slightly cooler wet season between May and August and a hot, dry season between September and April. The Brazilian highlands and plateaus of the South-east and Centre-west have distinct seasons, with cool, wet winters and hot, dry summers. The very south of the country experiences four seasons similar to those in northern Italy.

▲ *Caiman alligators in the Pantanal. This is the largest wetland area in the world – during the rainy season, most of it is underwater.*

THE HOME OF...

The Pantanal

The Pantanal is a vast wetland, which becomes one huge lake the size of France during the wet season. The main farming activity in the region is cattle ranching, and the area is important for waterfowl such as scarlet ibis and cormorant. There are also large numbers of caimans, capybara (a giant rodent), marsh deer, jaguars and giant anteaters.

Environmental issues

As Brazil's economy develops and its population grows, the country is facing major environmental problems. More factories are causing increased air and water pollution. As more people come to live in Brazil's cities, increased traffic and waste is also causing more pollution. At the same time, parts of the Amazon rainforest, Cerrado and Atlantic forest have been destroyed. This has led to the extinction of some plants and animals, and is now changing the climate of Brazil.

▼ *Large parts of Amazon rainforest have been cleared to make way for plantations. Farming is a vital part of Brazil's economy, but the forest clearance is contributing to global warming.*

FAMOUS BRAZILIAN

Chico Mendes (1944–88)

A rubber-tapper called Chico Mendes became internationally famous when he tried to stop cattle ranchers cutting down the rainforest in a remote part of the Amazon. He was shot dead by ranchers on 22 December 1988. His death caused an outcry across the world.

Lungs of the world

The Amazon rainforest covers more than 6 million sq km (2.3 million sq miles). It is sometimes called 'the lungs of the world' because it helps keep the global climate stable. Plants in the Amazon rainforest absorb huge amounts of energy from the Sun and carbon dioxide (a greenhouse gas) from the air, and release oxygen. When the rainforest is cut down and burnt, carbon dioxide is released into the atmosphere, and scientists believe this is playing a part in global climate change. In addition to this, fewer trees means less oxygen is released into the air.

Preventing pollution

The Brazilian government has responded to the environmental problems by forcing new factories to be designed to produce less pollution. The government has also set up a network of national parks and reserves, covering 3.9 per cent of the country, to try to protect rare wildlife. Brazil now produces much of its energy from renewable sources, especially hydroelectric power and biofuels for cars.

▶ *This dam, built at the headwaters of the Tocantins River, is one of many new power stations built to produce electricity on tributaries of the Amazon River.*

GOING GLOBAL

Parts of the rainforest and much of the Cerrado are being destroyed to make way for soyabean plantations. There is a huge demand for soyabeans to feed people in China, as well as dairy cattle in Europe. The needs of other countries are therefore responsible for some of Brazil's environmental problems.

The first Brazilians were the Indians who lived in Amazonia and along the coast. No one knows how many Indians lived in Brazil before the Portuguese arrived in 1500, but it was believed to be millions. Today, there are around half a million Indians in Brazil, belonging to over 200 different tribes.

Slavery in Brazil

After the Portuguese found their way to Brazil in 1500, thousands of Portuguese people moved to the new colony and many of them married Brazilian Indians. The Portuguese transported millions of slaves from Africa to work on the plantations of sugar and other crops. This had a big effect on the structure of the global population. Africa lost millions of people, and black Africans became a major part of the Brazilian population.

▼ *The Kayopo tribe of Amazonian Indians have fought against deforestation so they can preserve their way of life.*

▲ *The multicultural population can be seen in many parts of Brazil, with descendants of black Africans, European immigrants and mixed-race people.*

FAMOUS BRAZILIANS

Zumbi (1655–95)

Zumbi was born into a community of escaped slaves, but was captured by the Portuguese when he was a child. He later escaped and led the fight against slavery in North-east Brazil until he was killed in 1695. Many black Brazilians still honour him as a great warrior and hero.

A varied population

Brazil is now the fifth most populated country in the world. There are Amazonian Indians living deep in the rainforest, descendants of the first people of South America. There are also the descendants of African slaves and European people. The mixed-race people from a combination of Indians, Europeans and black Africans are known as *pardos*. Over the last 100 years, immigrants from many different countries have also moved to Brazil, including people from China, Japan and Lebanon.

A young population

Brazil's population has grown rapidly over the last 50 years, and it now accounts for nearly half of the entire population of South America. Although the rate of growth has slowed in the past 10 years, Brazil's population is still growing by nearly two million people every year. The Brazilian population is very young compared to countries such as the USA, Japan or Germany – more than a quarter of Brazilians are under 14 years old. This may cause problems, because schools must be built to educate them and jobs must be found as they grow older.

GOING GLOBAL

There are thought to be between 130,000 and 160,000 Brazilians living in London. These people have taken their culture with them, and as a result there are numerous samba clubs there, and even *churrascarias*, a type of barbecue restaurant popular in Brazil.

▼ *A Brazilian carnival is celebrated on the streets of Islington, North London. The English capital has a large Brazilian population.*

Population density

In 2010, the population density of Brazil was 23.04 people per sq km (59 people per sq mile). However, there are huge differences in population density around the country. For example, 90 per cent of Brazilians live within 100 km (62 miles) of the Atlantic coast. São Paulo has a population density of over 3,650 people per sq km (9,495 people per sq mile), whereas in the Amazon region it can be as low as two people per sq km (five people per sq mile).

Moving to the cities

Fifty years ago, more than two-thirds of people in Brazil lived in the countryside. Today, more than 80 per cent live in towns or cities, having moved in search of work and better opportunities. There is a big divide between rich and poor in Brazil, and most of the big cities have slums known as *favelas*, where millions of people live in very poor conditions. Thousands of Brazilians have also left the country in the last 50 years, providing young workers in countries with ageing populations such as the UK and the USA.

▶ *People come to the cities to find work, but often cannot afford housing there, so instead they settle in slums called favelas that spring up on the outskirts of the cities.*

PLACE IN THE WORLD

Population: **205,716,890**

Percentage of world total: **2.9%**

World ranking: **5th**

Brazil's rich culture today has been influenced by Amazonian Indians, European colonizers and African slaves. In addition, waves of other immigrants from countries such as Germany, Italy, Lebanon and Japan have influenced Brazilian culture.

Music and dance

Brazil is famous around the world for its music and dance, especially the samba, which was influenced by the music of the African slaves. The samba has become extremely popular all over the world, and samba-dancing lessons are enjoyed in many different countries.

THE HOME OF...

Carnival

The Rio Carnival – a huge, colourful dance competition held in Rio de Janeiro – has become famous throughout the world. Dozens of samba schools compete against each other for a week in a specially constructed 'sambadrome'. The Carnival is well-known for its brightly dressed dancers and lively music.

▲ *During the world-famous Rio Carnival, people pack into specially built venues to watch the dancers in brightly coloured costumes.*

A passion for sport

Brazilians are great sports fans. The Brazilian national football team has won the World Cup five times – more than any other country – and introduced a unique style to the sport. Interest in Brazilian football skills has meant that many of the great European football clubs, such as Real Madrid in Spain and Manchester United in England, have Brazilians in their teams. Brazilians have also been prominent in Formula One motor racing, with drivers such as Ayrton Senna, Nelson Piquet and Felipe Massa.

IT STARTED HERE

The capoeira

Capoeira is an art form that combines martial art and dance. It was developed by African slaves on the sugar plantations. They were forbidden to fight one another, so they invented a type of ritual combat instead.

▼ *In the dance form capoeira, performers take it in turns to sing, play musical instruments or 'fight' in the middle of a circle.*

Family life

Brazilian family life has changed over the last half a century. Fifty years ago, the majority of Brazilian people lived in the countryside, often with – or close to – several generations of their family. Today the majority of Brazilians live in cities. Millions have moved there in search of work, often leaving their families behind in rural areas. Women make up an increasing number of workers and there are also more single-parent families than ever before.

THE HOME OF...

Brazil nuts

All Brazil nuts are still harvested from wild trees that are among the largest that grow in the Amazon rainforest. None of the nuts that are transported from Brazil and other South American countries are grown on plantations. Each Brazil nut we eat has been cracked by hand.

Changing diet

Food is an important part of the Brazilian culture, but feeding more than 200 million people is a major challenge. Beans, rice, coffee and manioc (a plant with an edible root) are the staple foods for millions of Brazilians. There are many regional variations, with African-style food popular in the North-east region and European-style cuisine, such as cheese and wine, in the south. Many Brazilian foods are popular around the world, including Brazil nuts and acai juice. However, fast foods such as burgers and processed foods are also becoming increasingly popular.

◄ *Fruit juice made from acai berries, which are grown in the Amazon region of Brazil, has become popular all over the world because people believe it has energy-boosting properties.*

Education

Education is free for all children up until the age of 14. However, many children do not complete their education as they may have to work or help their parents look after younger children. It is also free to attend university, but the majority of university students still come from private schools.

Freedom to choose religion

Brazil has the second largest number of Christians in the world after the USA. The largest religious group is Roman Catholic, although Protestants are a fast-growing group, representing around one-fifth of the population. The Brazilian constitution states that people have the right to follow a religion of their choosing. African Brazilians follow several religions, including Candomblé.

IT'S A FACT!

The Candomblé religion is the best known of the African religions in Brazil, where it has more than a million followers. They believe that everyone has a god (Orixa), which guides and protects them, and followers also worship several other traditional African gods. Candomblé rituals involve dancing and drumming.

▼ *Followers of the Afro-Brazilian religion Candomblé gather by the sea to make offerings to the sea goddess Iemanjá.*

Economy and trade

The Brazilian economy has grown rapidly over the last 10 years. Although the rate of growth slowed because of the global economic crisis in 2008, Brazil is still one of the most important trading countries in the world. It is likely to become even more significant in the near future because of its large reserves of natural resources.

▲ *A man tosses freshly harvested coffee beans on a modern coffee plantation.*

Agriculture

Fifty years ago, around half of Brazil's workforce worked in agriculture, but today only around 20 per cent are employed in the farming industry. Farming has changed greatly in Brazil. Huge, mechanized 'mega farms' have been established in the South-east and Centre-west regions of Brazil, and these produce millions of tonnes of food for people and animals. However, in some parts of Brazil, farms are still small and family-run. Soyabeans are the fastest-growing crop, because China has an increasing demand to help feed its 1.3 billion people, and a growing economy to pay for it.

GLOBAL LEADER

Farming
Brazil is one of the world's most important farming countries, producing cheap food for the world. It is the leading producer of sugar, coffee, oranges and beef.

Mining

Brazil is one of the six most important mining countries in the world, with large deposits of bauxite (for aluminium), copper, asbestos, tin and diamonds. This means that it has an influence on the world economy, as it can choose which countries it wants to trade with in the future. Mineral exports between China and Brazil rose by 525 per cent between 1999 and 2003. In 2006 the presidents of China and Brazil met to further their trade partnership and in 2009 China overtook the USA to become Brazil's largest trading partner.

Services

Services are parts of a country's economy that earn money without producing any product, such as tourism and banking. Today, this part of the Brazilian economy employs around two-thirds of the entire workforce.

IT STARTED HERE

Powered flight

Before what is generally considered to be the first powered air flight by the Wright Brothers in 1903, a Brazilian called Alberto Santos Dumont already had his own personal flying machine. He lived in France and was famous for flying to the shops and to visit friends. He also liked to dine at Maxim's restaurant in Paris, which he would regularly fly to, tying his small airship to a lamp post outside while he enjoyed his meal.

▼ *Copacabana beach in Rio de Janeiro is a major tourist attraction because of its white sands and lively beach life. All these visitors help boost Brazil's economy.*

Manufacturing

Brazil is a major manufacturing nation, producing a huge range of goods, including vehicles, steel, textiles and footwear. Many foreign companies, including the US company Ford and the German company Volkswagen, run factories in Brazil, providing employment for many Brazilian people. In 2000, 14 of the 20 largest companies in Brazil were owned by foreign companies. Brazil ranks sixth in the world for car production.

Imports and exports

The rapid growth in Brazil's economy over the last 10 years is largely due to the increase in the goods and services that it exports to other countries. For example, the value of Brazil's exports rose by almost five times from 2001 to 2011, from US$58 billion to US$250.8 billion. At the same time imports grew from US$56 billion to US$219.6 billion. The main goods that Brazil imports are machinery, electrical equipment and chemical products.

▼ *Workers weld car frames on an assembly line in Sao Caetano do Sul, in a factory owned by US company General Motors.*

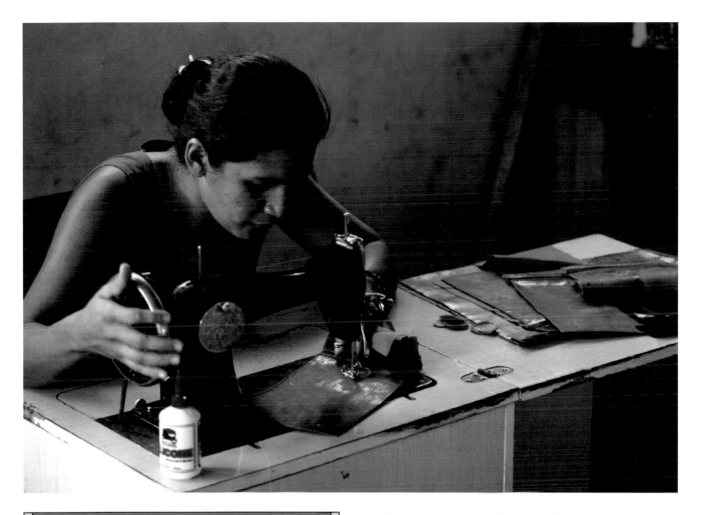

▲ *This woman is making handbags from imitation leather – actually rubber. This is part of a scheme to make money from the rainforest without destroying it.*

IT STARTED HERE

Rubber

Without the discovery and production of rubber, the world's motor industry could have had a very different history. The Portuguese first discovered the Omagua Amazonian Indians using the latex from the rubber tree to waterproof items. By the end of the nineteenth century, rubber had become a multi-million pound global industry.

Trading partners

Brazil's largest single trading partner is China, which accounted for 15.2 per cent of all exports in 2010. China replaced the USA, Brazil's largest trading partner since the 1930s. In 2010 the USA accounted for 9.6 per cent of all exports, Argentina accounted for 9.2 per cent, the Netherlands 5.1 per cent and Germany 4 per cent.

Brazil was a colony of Portugal for more than 300 years, which meant that the country was mainly run for the benefit of Portugal. This ended with Brazilian independence in 1822, but it was still many years before the country became the republic it is today.

From empire to republic

After 1822 Brazil was ruled by emperors, but in 1889 there was a military revolt and the emperor, Pedro II, stepped down. Brazil was declared a republic, but really the military controlled the country. Although there was a period of civilian rule, the army took over again in 1964 and it was not until 1985 that Brazil became a true republic.

The Brazilian government

Today, Brazil is a presidential republic like the USA. This means that the president is both head of the government and head of state. He is elected directly by the people. Brazil has 26 states, and each one elects its own local government. The National Congress has a president, a federal senate with 81 members, and a 513-seat chamber of deputies.

▼ *The National Congress of Brazil, in the capital Brasilia, was designed by world-famous Brazilian architect Oscar Niemeyer.*

▲ *Children greet a mascot at the 1992 Earth Summit (see box, below) to address global environmental problems.*

A new direction

In 2003, President Lula da Silva came to power. Almost immediately he tried to find ways to reduce the huge gap between rich and poor in Brazil. He changed Brazilian foreign policy, deciding that it was not good for Brazil to rely too much on Europe and the USA for overseas trade. Instead he began making trade agreements with other developing nations, including China. In 2011 President Lula da Silva stepped down to be replaced by Brazil's first female president, Dilma Rousseff.

IT STARTED HERE

The Earth Summit

The first Earth Summit was held in Rio de Janeiro in 1992. This meeting of United Nations countries was intended to work out ways to solve global environmental problems. Representatives from 172 nations attended the summit, and it influenced environmental policies all over the world.

By 2020, Brazil's population may have reached 210 million. Compared to countries in Europe and North America, it will still have a young population and a large workforce, which will give it an economic advantage over countries with older populations. However, there is the potential for unrest because of the huge gap between rich and poor in Brazil.

Boom or bust?

Many developing nations may face economic problems because they are using up too many of their natural resources. This is unlikely to happen in Brazil because it has such large reserves of so many resources that it will be able to provide its industries with the materials they need. This may mean it has an increasing influence on the global economy.

GLOBAL LEADER

Biofuels

After World War II (1939–45), the Brazilian government decided that it wanted to reduce its imports such as oil. It developed an industry producing alcohol from sugar cane (biofuel) for cars. Today, Brazil is a world leader in biofuel production, and around 20 per cent of Brazilian vehicles run on biofuel.

◀ *This man is harvesting sugar cane, which will be used as a biofuel. This fuel is cheap to produce and less polluting than petrol or diesel.*

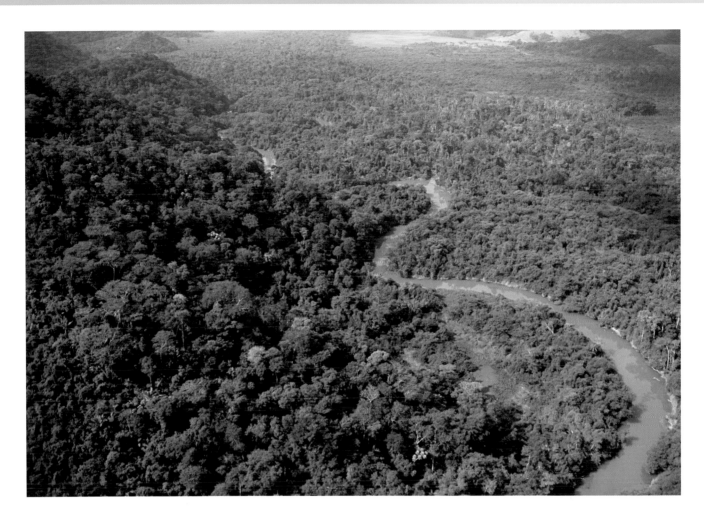

Deforestation and climate change

Brazil could suffer from environmental disaster if some of the major problems are not addressed. Deforestation in the Amazon is causing changes in weather patterns in Brazil and across the world. A change in temperature or rainfall in the large agricultural areas could be disastrous for crops. Also, some cities are already using more water than is locally available. However, Brazil has huge potential for producing renewable energy such as hydroelectric power, solar power and biofuel.

▲ *Limiting deforestation in the rainforests, while still developing its economy, is the most pressing problem Brazil faces in the near future.*

IT'S A FACT!

Brazil overtook the UK at the end of 2011 to become the sixth largest economy in the world. With its abundance of natural resources and large population, it is well-placed to maintain a strong position in the world economies.

Glossary

biofuel a fuel usually made from a plant material, such as wheat for ethanol.

Candomblé a religion practised in Brazil that has African origins.

Capoeira a type of slow-motion dancing and fighting developed by African slaves in Brazil.

churrascaria a type of barbecue restaurant that originated in Brazil but is now popular all over the world.

constitution the agreed general principles of a formal organization such as a national government.

drainage basin an area of land that contributes water to a stream or river.

economy the financial system of a country or region, including how much money is made from the production and sale of goods and services.

export to send or transport products, materials or services abroad for sale or trade.

extinction the dying out of a particular species of plant or animal.

favelas a Brazilian word for slums or shanty towns, which are often found on the outskirts of the big cities.

global warming the gradual rise in temperatures on the surface of the Earth caused by changes in the amount of greenhouse gases in the atmosphere.

greenhouse gas any of several gases that trap warmth in the atmosphere, which can contribute to global warming if too much is generated on Earth.

import to bring in goods or materials from a foreign country for sale.

manioc a root crop like a potato or a yam, which originally grew in the Amazon but is now grown industrially. Also known as cassava.

pardos a word describing mixed-race Brazilian people with white, black and Indian ancestry.

Planalto a high plateau in the Centre-west region of Brazil.

plantation a large area where crops such as coffee or sugar cane are grown in orderly rows.

rainforest a forest that receives more than 1 m (3.3 ft) of rainfall spread evenly throughout the year.

republic a political system whose head of state is not a king or queen, but a president who has been elected by the people.

resources things that are available to use, often to help develop a country's industry and economy. Resources could be minerals, workers (labour) or water.

Sertão a large area of semi-desert in the North-east region of Brazil.

Further information

Books

Changing World: Brazil
by Nicola Barber
(Franklin Watts, 2010)

The Changing Face of Brazil
by Edward Parker
(Wayland, 2007)

Travel Through: Brazil
by Joe Fullman
(QED Publishing, 2007)

Brazil (Destination Detectives)
by Ali Brownlie Bojang
(Raintree, 2007)

Countries of the World: Brazil
by Brian Dicks
(Evans Brothers, 2002/2005)

Websites

http://news.bbc.co.uk/1/hi/world/americas/country_profiles/1227110.stm
This is the BBC news page for Brazil, with recent events and background information including a timeline of major events.

https://www.cia.gov/library/publications/the-world-factbook/geos/br.html
A good source of general statistics about Brazil.

http://www.brazil.org.uk
The Brazilian embassy in the UK.

http://www.saopaulo.sp.gov.br/
The website of the São Paulo State government.

http://www.governo.rj.gov.br
Information on Rio de Janeiro.

Every effort has been made by the publisher to ensure that these websites contain no inappropriate or offensive material. However, because of the nature of the Internet, it is impossible to guarantee that the contents of these sites will not be altered. We strongly advise that Internet access is supervised by a responsible adult.

Index

Numbers in **bold** indicate pictures